NEEDS AND WANTS

by Marne Ventura

Cody Koala

An Imprint of Pop!
popbooksonline.com

abdopublishing.com
Published by Pop!, a division of ABDO, PO Box 398166, Minneapolis, Minnesota 55439. Copyright © 2019 by POP, LLC. International copyrights reserved in all countries. No part of this book may be reproduced in any form without written permission from the publisher. Pop!™ is a trademark and logo of POP, LLC.

Printed in the United States of America, North Mankato, Minnesota

032018
092018

THIS BOOK CONTAINS RECYCLED MATERIALS

Cover Photo: Shutterstock Images
Interior Photos: Shutterstock Images, 5 (top), 5 (bottom left), 5 (bottom right), 6, 9 (top), 9 (bottom left), 9 (bottom right), 10, 13, 14 (top right), 14 (top middle), 14 (bottom left), 16, 19 (bottom left), 19 (bottom right); iStockphoto, 14 (top left), 14 (bottom middle), 19 (top), 20

Editor: Charly Haley
Series Designer: Laura Mitchell

Library of Congress Control Number: 201796337
Publisher's Cataloging-in-Publication Data

Names: Ventura, Marne, author.
Title: Needs and wants / by Marne Ventura.
Description: Minneapolis, Minnesota : Pop!, 2019. | Series: Community economics |
Includes online resources and index.
Identifiers: ISBN 9781532160042 (lib.bdg.) | ISBN 9781532161162 (ebook) |
Subjects: LCSH: Basic needs--Juvenile literature. | Community development--Juvenile literature. | Regional economics--Juvenile literature. | Economic development--Juvenile literature. | Community life--Juvenile literature.
Classification: DDC 330.9--dc23

Hello! My name is

Cody Koala

Pop open this book and you'll find QR codes like this one, loaded with information, so you can learn even more!

Scan this code* and others like it while you read, or visit the website below to make this book pop.

popbooksonline.com/needs-and-wants

*Scanning QR codes requires a web-enabled smart device with a QR code reader app and a camera.

Table of Contents

Needs

A **need** is something that people must have to live. Food, shelter, and clothing are needs.

Watch a video here!

Clean air and water are needs. **Medical care** is a need.

> People everywhere have a lot of the same needs.

Wants

A **want** is something that people enjoy. Toys, desserts, and televisions are wants.

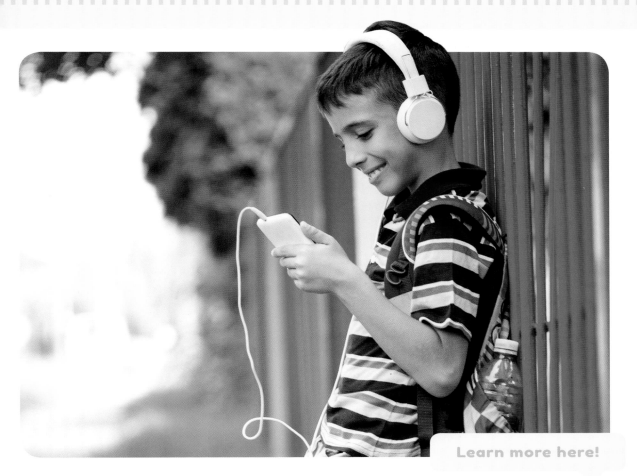

Learn more here!

People like having them. But people do not need them to live.

Chapter 3

Needs Before Wants

People use money to buy the things they need and want. Most people buy needs first. They pay for food, a place to live, and clothes.

Learn more here!

Needs

shelter   **food**   **water**

Wants

toys   **TV**   **jewelry**

Sometimes people have money left after paying for their needs. They might use that money for their wants. Or they might save some money for later.

People can share their money, food, or other things with people who can't pay for their own needs. This is called donating to charity.

Charities can help pay for someone's food, shelter, or medical bills.

Chapter 4

Making Choices

James's mom gives him $5. James needs to buy lunch at school. The lunch costs $2.50. James can choose how to spend the rest of the money.

Complete an activity here!

James wants a new game that costs $20. He saves his extra money. He buys the game when he has saved $20.

Making Connections

Text-to-Self

Think of the things that your family buys. Which of these things are needs? Which of them are wants?

Text-to-Text

Pick a character from your favorite book. What are the wants and needs of that character?

Text-to-World

What are some of the wants and needs of people around you?

Glossary

charity – a place that collects money or things to give to people who can't pay for their own needs.

medical care – going to a doctor when you are hurt or sick.

need – something that a person must have to live.

want – something that a person likes to have but can live without.

Index

Online Resources

popbooksonline.com

Thanks for reading this Cody Koala book!

Scan this code* and others like it in this book, or visit the website below to make this book pop!

popbooksonline.com/needs-and-wants

*Scanning QR codes requires a web-enabled smart device with a QR code reader app and a camera.